ISBN: 978-1-54398-002-8

THE STROKE
THAT TOUCHED MY *Heart*

GRATITUDE JOURNAL

---

*An Introduction to the
Transformative Power
of Gratitude Journaling*

MIA & MYRTLE RUSSELL

*Sometimes you don't realize
the weight of something
you've been carrying
until you feel
the weight of its release.*

10 Reasons To Start A Gratitude Journal:

1. It is based on the principle that small changes lead to big results. Gratitude gradually transforms you from the inside out. Like the caterpillar that slowly morphs into a butterfly, you shed old beliefs and begin to see what is important; you begin to put things in proper perspective.

2. To be grateful forces you to focus on what you have rather than what you don't have. Not only do you count your blessings, but you also begin to make your blessings count. Gratitude turns small things into big ones and a lack of gratitude causes big things to disappear.

3. A gratitude journal serves as a daily inventory of your blessings that causes your faith in divine goodness to grow stronger. The more faith you have in divine goodness, the more blessings you experience. Grateful people have hope in what will be, faith in the unseen, and gratitude for what is.

4. It teaches you to stop waiting for special days. Instead, you begin to look for what is special in each day.

5. It reduces stress and you feel more at peace. You learn to focus on the positives rather than the negatives and expect the best.

6. Grateful people are easy to recognize: they are happier, healthier, energizing, and a joy to be around.

7. It helps you realize that the will of God is good, and sometimes the only thing that stands in the way of you and your good is you.

8. It helps you understand abundance, recognize miracles, and embrace prosperity. You begin to tap into your inner power and allow that power to guide you.

9. It generates ideas and encourages creativity. Had I not kept a journal, these books would never have been written.

10. Gratitude leads to a life of service. When you realize how much you have to be thankful for, you just cannot keep it all to yourself; you have to share it. To serve those in need is like receiving more gifts for yourself. Why?

Because giving and receiving are two sides of the same coin. Grateful people learn to serve and be served!

"Sometimes," Sylvie said, "one can mistake gratitude for love."
-Kate Atkinson

Designed as a companion to The Stroke That Touched My Heart (2019, BookBaby.com) this book introduces gratitude journaling by offering the reader daily prompts to get started. Together the two books put you on the road to living a more meaningful life through gratitude and journaling, regardless of the circumstances.

Grab your pen, sign the gratitude commitment below, and let the transformation begin!

Gratitude Commitment:

I _____ commit to making the small change to spend at least 30 minutes each day for the next 117 days writing in my gratitude journal, using The Stroke That Touched My Heart to get me started. I understand that I have plenty of time to journal because each day brings me 1,440 minutes and I deserve to spend 30 of those minutes focusing on me and gratitude. I believe that this small change is the beginning of me living a more fulfilled life.

In order to prevent isolation and receive the support I need, I will solicit the help of a trusted friend or mentor to witness this contract. By signing as a witness, (S)he agrees to encourage me to take responsibility for accomplishing my goals and hold me accountable along this journey.

Signature _____ Date _____

Witness Signature _____ Date _____

Intuition

YOUR GRATITUDE STORY: Divine intuition always has your best interest at heart and can come in different forms. It may be a feeling or a knowing that you can't ignore; a dream, a physical sign, a hunch, or a gut reaction.

Describe a time when you followed your intuition. How did it make you feel?

_____

_____

_____

_____

_____

_____

_____

List 10 things you are grateful for today.

_____

_____

_____

_____

_____

_____

_____

_____

_____

_____

Day 2

Emergency Medical Technicians (EMT)

YOUR GRATITUDE STORY: List five reasons to be grateful for EMTs.

_____

_____

_____

_____

_____

_____

_____

_____

_____

_____

List 10 things you are grateful for today.

_____

_____

_____

_____

_____

_____

_____

_____

_____

_____

Emergency Rooms (ER)

YOUR GRATITUDE STORY: List five things that emergency room personnel do that you can't do.

_____

_____

_____

_____

_____

_____

_____

_____

_____

List 10 things you are grateful for today.

_____

_____

_____

_____

_____

_____

_____

_____

_____

_____

Day 4

Prayer

YOUR GRATITUDE STORY: Want to let go of your worries? Try this worry game: Buy yourself a good sized jar and label it "My Worry Jar." Keep it in a private place. Each time something begins to bother you, grab a small piece of paper, write it down, fold it, put it in the jar, and leave it there. Say to yourself, "I'm leaving this worry to a higher power." Then move on with your day. Keep doing it every time a new worry comes about. After a period of time, say six months to a year, see how many prayers were answered, how many worries were forgotten. You will also discover that about half of what you worried about never happened, so why allow it to steal your joy? Go ahead and write one worry below.

_____

_____

_____

_____

List 10 things you are grateful for today. Don't forget to list your "worry jar."

_____

_____

_____

_____

_____

_____

_____

_____

_____

_____

Day 5

Hope

YOUR GRATITUDE STORY: List one thing you hope for and describe what you are doing to keep your hope from dying.

_____

_____

_____

_____

_____

_____

_____

_____

_____

List 10 things you are grateful for today.

_____

_____

_____

_____

_____

_____

_____

_____

_____

Diagnostic Tests

YOUR GRATITUDE STORY: Look around your home. What are five inventions that you wouldn't want to live without?

_____

_____

_____

_____

_____

_____

_____

_____

_____

_____

List 10 things you are grateful for today.

_____

_____

_____

_____

_____

_____

_____

_____

_____

A Craniectomy

YOUR GRATITUDE STORY: What medical invention(s) have you or a loved one had to use and how has it improved your life?

_____

_____

_____

_____

_____

_____

_____

_____

_____

_____

List 10 things you are grateful for today.

_____

_____

_____

_____

_____

_____

_____

_____

_____

_____

A Neurosurgeon's "Piece Of Cake"

YOUR GRATITUDE STORY: List five reasons you are glad to be alive.

_____

_____

_____

_____

_____

_____

_____

_____

_____

_____

_____

_____

List 10 things you are grateful for today.

_____

_____

_____

_____

_____

_____

_____

_____

_____

_____

_____

Joy

YOUR GRATITUDE STORY: Joy is an inside job. Write about at least one thing that ignites the joy in you.

_____

_____

_____

_____

_____

_____

_____

_____

_____

_____

List 10 things you are grateful for today.

_____

_____

_____

_____

_____

_____

_____

_____

_____

_____

Good Luck Charms

YOUR GRATITUDE STORY: What good luck charm(s) do you use? Why?

_____

_____

_____

_____

_____

_____

_____

_____

_____

List 10 things you are grateful for today.

_____

_____

_____

_____

_____

_____

_____

_____

Insurance

YOUR GRATITUDE STORY: List five guarantees you have in life, things you know for sure.

_____

_____

_____

_____

_____

_____

_____

_____

_____

List 10 things you are grateful for today.

_____

_____

_____

_____

_____

_____

_____

_____

_____

Helmets

YOUR GRATITUDE STORY: Finish this sentence: One little thing that has made a big difference in my life is _____

_____

_____

_____

_____

_____

_____

_____

_____

_____

List 10 things you are grateful for today.

_____

_____

_____

_____

_____

_____

_____

_____

_____

Day 13

Encouraging Words

YOUR GRATITUDE STORY: Who is the last person that delivered encouraging words to you? What were they? Did you thank her/him?

_____

_____

_____

_____

_____

_____

_____

_____

_____

_____

List 10 things you are grateful for today.

_____

_____

_____

_____

_____

_____

_____

_____

The World Wide Web

YOUR GRATITUDE STORY: List five ways you benefit from using the Internet.

_____

_____

_____

_____

_____

_____

_____

_____

_____

_____

List 10 things you are grateful for today.

_____

_____

_____

_____

_____

_____

_____

_____

_____

_____

Classmates

YOUR GRATITUDE STORY: Think of five things you can do to cheer someone else up. Do one each week for five weeks and see how good it makes you feel.

_____

_____

_____

_____

_____

_____

_____

_____

_____

List 10 things you are grateful for today.

_____

_____

_____

_____

_____

_____

_____

_____

_____

Vigilance

YOUR GRATITUDE STORY: List five things you like most about yourself. How can you use them to help others?

_____

_____

_____

_____

_____

_____

_____

_____

_____

_____

List 10 things you are grateful for today.

_____

_____

_____

_____

_____

_____

_____

_____

A Time To Search

YOUR GRATITUDE STORY: What do you do when you have questions you can't answer? Here's a suggestion: Put them in your "worry jar." Each time they pop into your head, keep writing them down. The answers will come but you have to be paying attention to recognize them. Write your questions below.

_____

_____

_____

_____

_____

_____

_____

_____

_____

List 10 things you are grateful for today.

_____

_____

_____

_____

_____

_____

_____

_____

_____

_____

Home Remedies

YOUR GRATITUDE STORY: What home remedies have you used that worked?

_____

_____

_____

_____

_____

_____

_____

_____

_____

_____

List 10 things you are grateful for today.

_____

_____

_____

_____

_____

_____

_____

_____

_____

_____

Laughter

YOUR GRATITUDE STORY: List five things or five people that always make you laugh.

_____

_____

_____

_____

_____

_____

_____

_____

_____

List 10 things you are grateful for today.

_____

_____

_____

_____

_____

_____

_____

_____

_____

Big Brothers

YOUR GRATITUDE STORY: How many siblings do you have? List one special thing you like about each one of them.

_____

_____

_____

_____

_____

_____

_____

_____

_____

_____

List 10 things you are grateful for today.

_____

_____

_____

_____

_____

_____

_____

_____

_____

A Dying Friend

YOUR GRATITUDE STORY: If you could bring back three people from the dead, who would they be and why?

_____

_____

_____

_____

_____

_____

_____

_____

_____

_____

List 10 things you are grateful for today.

_____

_____

_____

_____

_____

_____

_____

_____

_____

_____

Answers

YOUR GRATITUDE STORY: Think of a time when you experienced a crisis. Who were the people that stepped in to help you get through it? Did you thank them? It's not too late you know. Even if they are no longer alive, write them a "thank you" note. It feels good.

_____

_____

_____

_____

_____

_____

_____

_____

List 10 things you are grateful for today.

_____

_____

_____

_____

_____

_____

_____

_____

_____

Social Security Disability Benefits

YOUR GRATITUDE STORY: List five ways you have ever benefited from government services.

_____

_____

_____

_____

_____

_____

_____

_____

_____

_____

List 10 things you are grateful for today.

_____

_____

_____

_____

_____

_____

_____

_____

_____

_____

Student Loans

YOUR GRATITUDE STORY: Use the Internet to find five countries that do not offer student loans, countries where education has to be paid for out-of-pocket.

_____

_____

_____

_____

_____

_____

_____

_____

_____

List 10 things you are grateful for today.

_____

_____

_____

_____

_____

_____

_____

_____

_____

_____

Taxes

YOUR GRATITUDE STORY: Everyone who has worked and paid taxes has an IRS story. What's yours? Did it have a happy or sad ending? Remember, there's something to be grateful for in both.

_____

_____

_____

_____

_____

_____

_____

_____

_____

List 10 things you are grateful for today.

_____

_____

_____

_____

_____

_____

_____

_____

_____

_____

Assistive Devices

YOUR GRATITUDE STORY: Almost everyone will need at least one assistive device in their lifetime. List the assistive devices you use now or have had to use in the past.

_____

_____

_____

_____

_____

_____

_____

_____

_____

_____

List 10 things you are grateful for today.

_____

_____

_____

_____

_____

_____

_____

_____

_____

_____

Valentines

YOUR GRATITUDE STORY: If you had a million dollars that you had to give away, list five people or organizations you would give it to? Why?

_____

_____

_____

_____

_____

_____

_____

_____

_____

List 10 things you are grateful for today.

_____

_____

_____

_____

_____

_____

_____

_____

_____

Jigsaw Puzzles

YOUR GRATITUDE STORY: If you could design a jigsaw puzzle of one person, who would it be? How many pieces would your puzzle consist of?

_____

_____

_____

_____

_____

_____

_____

_____

_____

List 10 things you are grateful for today.

_____

_____

_____

_____

_____

_____

_____

_____

_____

_____

Disappointment

YOUR GRATITUDE STORY: What has been one of your greatest disappointments? What lesson did you learn from it?

_____

_____

_____

_____

_____

_____

_____

_____

_____

List 10 things you are grateful for today.

_____

_____

_____

_____

_____

_____

_____

_____

_____

Resources

YOUR GRATITUDE STORY: List five things you would like to do before you die. What's stopping you from doing them?

_____

_____

_____

_____

_____

_____

_____

_____

_____

List 10 things you are grateful for today.

_____

_____

_____

_____

_____

_____

_____

_____

_____

Social Workers

YOUR GRATITUDE STORY: Reach out to a social worker, any social worker, and thank her/ him for their service. If you think you don't know any, start with any social service agency like the Department of Human Services (DHS) or the Department of Children's Services (DCS). Social workers rarely get the thanks they deserve. Don't forget to journal about how good it made you feel to reach out.

_____

_____

_____

_____

_____

_____

List 10 things you are grateful for today.

_____

_____

_____

_____

_____

_____

_____

_____

_____

Goodbyes

YOUR GRATITUDE STORY: What's the hardest "goodbye" you ever had to make? Describe it. Every "goodbye" is a new beginning. Describe the new beginning as well.

_____

_____

_____

_____

_____

_____

_____

_____

_____

_____

List 10 things you are grateful for today.

_____

_____

_____

_____

_____

_____

_____

_____

_____

_____

Motorized Shopping Carts

YOUR GRATITUDE STORY: Have you ever made unkind remarks about people on motorized shopping carts? The next time you see someone using a motorized shopping cart, don't judge. You don't know their story. Offer to help instead. What are some ways you could help a person using a motorized shopping cart? What help would you need if you had to use one?

_____

_____

_____

_____

_____

_____

List 10 things you are grateful for today.

_____

_____

_____

_____

_____

_____

_____

_____

Acts Of Kindness

YOUR GRATITUDE STORY: For a week, do something kind for seven different people and each day journal about how it felt.

_____

_____

_____

_____

_____

_____

_____

_____

_____

_____

List 10 things you are grateful for today.

_____

_____

_____

_____

_____

_____

_____

_____

_____

_____

Outpatient Therapists

YOUR GRATITUDE STORY: List three people that you absolutely know care about you. Do something to let them know that you appreciate them before it's too late.

_____

_____

_____

_____

_____

_____

_____

_____

_____

List 10 things you are grateful for today.

_____

_____

_____

_____

_____

_____

_____

_____

_____

Mix- Matched Shoes

YOUR GRATITUDE STORY: List three compliments you receive on a regular basis. How many of them have to do with your physical appearance? How do you react when you are complimented?

_____

_____

_____

_____

_____

_____

_____

_____

_____

_____

List 10 things you are grateful for today.

_____

_____

_____

_____

_____

_____

_____

_____

_____

_____

"Thank You" Notes

YOUR GRATITUDE STORY: Fill in the blank: I feel grateful when

_____

_____

_____

_____

_____

_____

_____

_____

_____

_____

List 10 things you are grateful for today.

_____

_____

_____

_____

_____

_____

_____

_____

_____

A Shower

YOUR GRATITUDE STORY: How would your life change if you couldn't take a shower or bath for a week, a month, two months?

_____

_____

_____

_____

_____

_____

_____

_____

_____

List 10 things you are grateful for today.

_____

_____

_____

_____

_____

_____

_____

_____

Remembering The Stroke

YOUR GRATITUDE STORY: List five things or people you want to remember for as long as you live.

_____

_____

_____

_____

_____

_____

_____

_____

_____

List 10 things you are grateful for today.

_____

_____

_____

_____

_____

_____

_____

_____

_____

Learning To Write My Name

YOUR GRATITUDE STORY: List one kindergarten lesson you never forgot. Why is it easy to remember?

_____

_____

_____

_____

_____

_____

_____

_____

_____

_____

List 10 things you are grateful for today.

_____

_____

_____

_____

_____

_____

_____

_____

_____

Medical Bills And Bad Credit

YOUR GRATITUDE STORY: Make a list of everyone you owe and why you owe them. For each one that you owe, say thank you.

_____

_____

_____

_____

_____

_____

_____

_____

_____

_____

List 10 things you are grateful for today.

_____

_____

_____

_____

_____

_____

_____

Choices

YOUR GRATITUDE STORY: Describe one time that your patience was tested. How did things turn out?

_____

_____

_____

_____

_____

_____

_____

_____

_____

_____

List 10 things you are grateful for today.

_____

_____

_____

_____

_____

_____

_____

_____

_____

Co-Workers

YOUR GRATITUDE STORY: Write about a time that you received help from compassionate co-workers. Write about a time when you have been a compassionate co-worker.

_____

_____

_____

_____

_____

_____

_____

_____

_____

_____

List 10 things you are grateful for today.

_____

_____

_____

_____

_____

_____

_____

_____

_____

Change

YOUR GRATITUDE STORY: What is one change you've had to adjust to over the last year? What lesson did you learn from it?

_____

_____

_____

_____

_____

_____

_____

_____

_____

_____

List 10 things you are grateful for today.

_____

_____

_____

_____

_____

_____

_____

_____

_____

_____

Her Daddy's Genes

YOUR GRATITUDE STORY: What genes from your parents are you most proud of?

_____

_____

_____

_____

_____

_____

_____

_____

_____

List 10 things you are grateful for today.

_____

_____

_____

_____

_____

_____

_____

_____

Reflections

YOUR GRATITUDE STORY: Complete this sentence: When it comes to my life, I totally understand _____

_____

_____

_____

_____

_____

_____

_____

_____

_____

List 10 things you are grateful for today.

_____

_____

_____

_____

_____

_____

_____

_____

Neuroplasticity

YOUR GRATITUDE STORY: Complete this sentence: I have been wanting to _____

_____

for a long time, but never did because _____

_____

_____

_____

_____

_____

_____

_____

_____

List 10 things you are grateful for today.

_____

_____

_____

_____

_____

_____

_____

_____

Patience

YOUR GRATITUDE STORY: Describe a time when you had to wait for something. How did it make you feel and how did things turn out?

_____

_____

_____

_____

_____

_____

_____

_____

_____

_____

List 10 things you are grateful for today.

_____

_____

_____

_____

_____

_____

_____

_____

_____

Fear

YOUR GRATITUDE STORY: Fear cuts both ways. Describe one time that doing the thing you feared paid off. Describe one time that doing the thing you feared got you into trouble.

_____

_____

_____

_____

_____

_____

_____

_____

_____

List 10 things you are grateful for today.

_____

_____

_____

_____

_____

_____

_____

_____

_____

A Hard-Headed Fall

YOUR GRATITUDE STORY: Growing up, what catchy phrases did your parents use when you were "hard-headed?"

_____

_____

_____

_____

_____

_____

_____

_____

_____

List 10 things you are grateful for today.

_____

_____

_____

_____

_____

_____

_____

_____

_____

$6 Glasses

YOUR GRATITUDE STORY: What is one thing that you recently purchased that cost a lot but turned out to be of little value? What is one thing you recently purchased that cost a little and turned out to be of great value?

_____

_____

_____

_____

_____

_____

_____

_____

_____

List 10 things you are grateful for today.

_____

_____

_____

_____

_____

_____

_____

_____

_____

Sisters

YOUR GRATITUDE STORY: Describe a special bond you have with your sister (or someone you feel especially close to). Have you told them how special they are?

_____

_____

_____

_____

_____

_____

_____

_____

_____

List 10 things you are grateful for today.

_____

_____

_____

_____

_____

_____

_____

_____

_____

Is Age More Than A Number?

YOUR GRATITUDE STORY: What age would you be if you didn't know how old you were? Why would you choose that age?

_____

_____

_____

_____

_____

_____

_____

_____

_____

List 10 things you are grateful for today.

_____

_____

_____

_____

_____

_____

_____

_____

Day 54

A Center For The Disabled

YOUR GRATITUDE STORY: Describe a time when you expected the best and the best followed.

_____

_____

_____

_____

_____

_____

_____

_____

_____

_____

List 10 things you are grateful for today.

_____

_____

_____

_____

_____

_____

_____

_____

Bedtime Stories

YOUR GRATITUDE STORY: When was the last time you read a good story that changed the way you felt or inspired you to act on something you've been putting off doing?

_____

_____

_____

_____

_____

_____

_____

_____

List 10 things you are grateful for today.

_____

_____

_____

_____

_____

_____

_____

_____

Smart Phones

YOUR GRATITUDE STORY: List five good things that having a smart phone enables you to do.

_____

_____

_____

_____

_____

_____

_____

_____

_____

_____

List 10 things you are grateful for today.

_____

_____

_____

_____

_____

_____

_____

_____

_____

_____

A Fanny Pack

YOUR GRATITUDE STORY: List five things in your wallet you would hate to lose. Where would you carry them if you didn't have a wallet?

_____

_____

_____

_____

_____

_____

_____

_____

_____

List 10 things you are grateful for today.

_____

_____

_____

_____

_____

_____

_____

_____

_____

Good News

YOUR GRATITUDE STORY: Describe the last piece of good news you received. How did you show gratitude when you received it?

_____

_____

_____

_____

_____

_____

_____

_____

_____

_____

List 10 things you are grateful for today.

_____

_____

_____

_____

_____

_____

_____

_____

_____

_____

Gratitude Journaling

YOUR GRATITUDE STORY: Most regrets expressed by individuals at the end of life are regrets for things they didn't do. List at least three things you feel you must do before you die. Now journal about what holds you back.

_____

_____

_____

_____

_____

_____

_____

List 10 things you are grateful for today.

_____

_____

_____

_____

_____

_____

_____

_____

A Seizure

YOUR GRATITUDE STORY: Usually our worries stem from thinking about something that happened in the past or something that is going to happen in the future. Describe a time when you thought the worst but the worst never happened.

_____

_____

_____

_____

_____

_____

_____

List 10 things you are grateful for today.

_____

_____

_____

_____

_____

_____

_____

_____

_____

Something To Sing About

YOUR GRATITUDE STORY: List five good things that you have to sing about. Were they things you did for someone else or things that were done for you?

_____

_____

_____

_____

_____

_____

_____

_____

List 10 things you are grateful for today.

_____

_____

_____

_____

_____

_____

_____

_____

_____

Birds On The Line

YOUR GRATITUDE STORY: List five milestones in your life, big or small.

_____

_____

_____

_____

_____

_____

_____

_____

_____

List 10 things you are grateful for today.

_____

_____

_____

_____

_____

_____

_____

_____

_____

Closed Doors And Opened Windows

YOUR GRATITUDE STORY: Describe a time when you acted on faith and it turned out to be a major turning point in your life.

_____

_____

_____

_____

_____

_____

_____

_____

_____

_____

List 10 things you are grateful for today.

_____

_____

_____

_____

_____

_____

_____

_____

_____

Supplemental Security Income

YOUR GRATITUDE STORY: More things are accomplished by prayer than the world realizes. List five prayers you've had answered.

_____

_____

_____

_____

_____

_____

_____

_____

_____

_____

List 10 things you are grateful for today.

_____

_____

_____

_____

_____

_____

_____

_____

_____

_____

Good Grief!

YOUR GRATITUDE STORY: We all experience grief but we don't all express it in the same way. Want to express it in a healthy way? Write about it.

_____

_____

_____

_____

_____

_____

_____

_____

List 10 things you are grateful for today.

_____

_____

_____

_____

_____

_____

_____

_____

Baby Steps

YOUR GRATITUDE STORY: List five things you've accomplished over the last ten years.

_____

_____

_____

_____

_____

_____

_____

_____

_____

List 10 things you are grateful for today.

_____

_____

_____

_____

_____

_____

_____

_____

_____

_____

Mothers

YOUR GRATITUDE STORY: List five reasons you are thankful for your mother.

_____

_____

_____

_____

_____

_____

_____

_____

_____

List 10 things you are grateful for today.

_____

_____

_____

_____

_____

_____

_____

_____

_____

Medicaid

YOUR GRATITUDE STORY: If you have health insurance, list five reasons you're grateful to have it. What would you have to be thankful for if you didn't have it?

_____

_____

_____

_____

_____

_____

_____

_____

_____

List 10 things you are grateful for today.

_____

_____

_____

_____

_____

_____

_____

_____

_____

Day 69

Bonds

YOUR GRATITUDE STORY: List five people with whom you have a strong bond. When you're finished, write them a note or give them a call to tell them how you feel about them.

_____

_____

_____

_____

_____

_____

_____

_____

List 10 things you are grateful for today.

_____

_____

_____

_____

_____

_____

_____

_____

_____

_____

Anger

YOUR GRATITUDE STORY: When is the last time you've been angry about something? Did it cause you to hurt someone's feelings? If so, did you apologize? If not, why?

_____

_____

_____

_____

_____

_____

_____

_____

_____

List 10 things you are grateful for today.

_____

_____

_____

_____

_____

_____

_____

_____

_____

_____

A Gratitude Story

YOUR GRATITUDE STORY: List your five favorite teachers. What made them different? Have you expressed your gratitude to them? If not, why not now? Even if they have died, still write them a thank you note in your journal.

_____

_____

_____

_____

_____

_____

_____

List 10 things you are grateful for today.

_____

_____

_____

_____

_____

_____

_____

_____

Anticipation

YOUR GRATITUDE STORY: What part of your body do you treasure the most? What would life be like without it?

_____

_____

_____

_____

_____

_____

_____

_____

_____

List 10 things you are grateful for today.

_____

_____

_____

_____

_____

_____

_____

_____

_____

A Good Barber

YOUR GRATITUDE STORY: Almost everyone has sat in the chair of a barber or stylist. List three things you like about your barber or stylist.

_____

_____

_____

_____

_____

_____

_____

_____

List 10 things you are grateful for today.

_____

_____

_____

_____

_____

_____

_____

_____

The Healing Power Of Music

YOUR GRATITUDE STORY: List three ways music improves your mood or makes life better.

_____

_____

_____

_____

_____

_____

_____

_____

_____

_____

List 10 things you are grateful for today.

_____

_____

_____

_____

_____

_____

_____

_____

_____

_____

Godmothers

YOUR GRATITUDE STORY: Everybody has a godmother story. Write about yours. Whether she is living or deceased, don't forget to thank her.

_____

_____

_____

_____

_____

_____

_____

_____

_____

List 10 things you are grateful for today.

_____

_____

_____

_____

_____

_____

_____

_____

Nostalgia

YOUR GRATITUDE STORY: What were your favorite childhood foods? How many do you still enjoy?

_____

_____

_____

_____

_____

_____

_____

_____

_____

_____

List 10 things you are grateful for today.

_____

_____

_____

_____

_____

_____

_____

_____

_____

_____

Two Brains

YOUR GRATITUDE STORY: List five ways that your life would change if suddenly your brain stopped working properly.

_____

_____

_____

_____

_____

_____

_____

_____

List 10 things you are grateful for today.

_____

_____

_____

_____

_____

_____

_____

_____

Uncles

YOUR GRATITUDE STORY: What uncle has made a difference in your life and how? When's the last time you thanked him?

_____

_____

_____

_____

_____

_____

_____

_____

_____

_____

List 10 things you are grateful for today.

_____

_____

_____

_____

_____

_____

_____

_____

_____

_____

Disappointment

YOUR GRATITUDE STORY: What has been one of your greatest disappointments? What lesson did you learn from it? How did you overcome it?

_____

_____

_____

_____

_____

_____

_____

_____

_____

List 10 things you are grateful for today.

_____

_____

_____

_____

_____

_____

_____

_____

_____

A Regular Cane

YOUR GRATITUDE STORY: Write about one of your proudest moments.

_____

_____

_____

_____

_____

_____

_____

_____

_____

List 10 things you are grateful for today.

_____

_____

_____

_____

_____

_____

_____

_____

Loyalty

YOUR GRATITUDE STORY: On a scale of 1-10, how loyal are you? Do you make promises that you don't keep? Write about a time when you were loyal and it paid off.

_____

_____

_____

_____

_____

_____

_____

_____

_____

List 10 things you are grateful for today.

_____

_____

_____

_____

_____

_____

_____

_____

_____

It Takes Two

YOUR GRATITUDE STORY: Who is the one person you can always count on? When was the last time you expressed your appreciation to that person?

_____

_____

_____

_____

_____

_____

_____

_____

_____

List 10 things you are grateful for today.

_____

_____

_____

_____

_____

_____

_____

_____

_____

_____

The Surgeon's Recovery

YOUR GRATITUDE STORY: List five people you pray for and why.

_____

_____

_____

_____

_____

_____

_____

_____

_____

_____

List 10 things you are grateful for today.

_____

_____

_____

_____

_____

_____

_____

_____

_____

_____

_____

Brownies

YOUR GRATITUDE STORY: List in your journal all the compliments you have ever received and beside each one, write the words "thank you."

_____

_____

_____

_____

_____

_____

_____

_____

_____

_____

List 10 things you are grateful for today.

_____

_____

_____

_____

_____

_____

_____

_____

_____

Getting Her Hard-Head Back

YOUR GRATITUDE STORY: List five good things that you have experienced today.

_____

_____

_____

_____

_____

_____

_____

_____

_____

_____

List 10 things you are grateful for today.

_____

_____

_____

_____

_____

_____

_____

_____

_____

_____

An Early Discharge

YOUR GRATITUDE STORY: What unexpected blessings have you experienced lately? What other people were involved? Did you thank them?

_____

_____

_____

_____

_____

_____

_____

_____

_____

_____

List 10 things you are grateful for today.

_____

_____

_____

_____

_____

_____

_____

_____

_____

My Battle Scar

YOUR GRATITUDE STORY: What battle scar(s) do you have? Write about it.

_____

_____

_____

_____

_____

_____

_____

_____

_____

List 10 things you are grateful for today.

_____

_____

_____

_____

_____

_____

_____

_____

Friendship

YOUR GRATITUDE STORY: List five qualities you love about your best friend. Thank her/him for sharing those qualities with you.

_____

_____

_____

_____

_____

_____

_____

_____

_____

List 10 things you are grateful for today.

_____

_____

_____

_____

_____

_____

_____

_____

Television

YOUR GRATITUDE STORY: List five of your favorite TV shows. After each one write "thank you _____ (your favorite actor/actress) for sharing your talent with me."

_____

_____

_____

_____

_____

_____

_____

_____

_____

List 10 things you are grateful for today.

_____

_____

_____

_____

_____

_____

_____

_____

_____

_____

Day 90

Love

YOUR GRATITUDE STORY: List one problem you have and how it can be solved through love.

_____

_____

_____

_____

_____

_____

_____

_____

_____

_____

List 10 things you are grateful for today.

_____

_____

_____

_____

_____

_____

_____

_____

_____

_____

Cradle Crap And Baby Oil

YOUR GRATITUDE STORY: Look around the room and list five things that cost less than a dollar. Less than $5. Less than $10. How have those things been a blessing to you?

_____

_____

_____

_____

_____

_____

_____

_____

_____

List 10 things you are grateful for today.

_____

_____

_____

_____

_____

_____

_____

_____

_____

Digital Clocks

YOUR GRATITUDE STORY: Are you a good time manager? How would you manage your time if you couldn't tell time?

_____

_____

_____

_____

_____

_____

_____

_____

_____

_____

List 10 things you are grateful for today.

_____

_____

_____

_____

_____

_____

_____

_____

_____

Index Cards

YOUR GRATITUDE STORY: Make a list of the positive thinkers you associate with. Make a list of the negative thinkers you associate with. With whom do you spend the most time?

_____

_____

_____

_____

_____

_____

_____

_____

_____

List 10 things you are grateful for today.

_____

_____

_____

_____

_____

_____

_____

_____

_____

A Lesson From An Old Friend

YOUR GRATITUDE STORY: If you had to live on a remote island for a year and could only take one person with you, who would you take and why?

_____

_____

_____

_____

_____

_____

_____

_____

_____

List 10 things you are grateful for today.

_____

_____

_____

_____

_____

_____

_____

_____

_____

"Cut Loose"

YOUR GRATITUDE STORY: List five things you have given away with no strings attached.

_____

_____

_____

_____

_____

_____

_____

_____

List 10 things you are grateful for today.

_____

_____

_____

_____

_____

_____

_____

_____

The Gift Of Giving

YOUR GRATITUDE STORY: List three of the best gifts you've ever given to yourself.

_____

_____

_____

_____

_____

_____

_____

_____

_____

_____

List 10 things you are grateful for today.

_____

_____

_____

_____

_____

_____

_____

_____

_____

Trust

YOUR GRATITUDE STORY: List five things you are 100 percent certain you can do.

_____

_____

_____

_____

_____

_____

_____

_____

_____

_____

List 10 things you are grateful for today.

_____

_____

_____

_____

_____

_____

_____

_____

_____

_____

Letting Go

YOUR GRATITUDE STORY: Name one crutch you have a hard time letting go of. Why?

_____

_____

_____

_____

_____

_____

_____

_____

_____

_____

List 10 things you are grateful for today.

_____

_____

_____

_____

_____

_____

_____

_____

_____

A Six-Month Pass

YOUR GRATITUDE STORY: Go back over your gratitude list and count the number of things you're grateful for since you started journaling. When you work on gratitude, gratitude works on you. Write down your favorites (if you can) and Keep Counting!

_____

_____

_____

_____

_____

_____

_____

_____

List 10 things you are grateful for today.

_____

_____

_____

_____

_____

_____

_____

_____

_____

_____

Day 100

Staying Awake All Day

YOUR GRATITUDE STORY: How many hours of sleep do you get each night? Is it too much or too little?

_____

_____

_____

_____

_____

_____

_____

_____

_____

List 10 things you are grateful for today.

_____

_____

_____

_____

_____

_____

_____

_____

_____

Day 101

College Homecoming

YOUR GRATITUDE STORY: When's the last time you attended any kind of "homecoming?" List five things you enjoyed.

_____

_____

_____

_____

_____

_____

_____

_____

_____

List 10 things you are grateful for today.

_____

_____

_____

_____

_____

_____

_____

_____

_____

Sharing Good Memories

YOUR GRATITUDE STORY: What is the last piece of good news you shared? Who did you share it with? What makes you feel better, sharing good news or bad news?

_____

_____

_____

_____

_____

_____

_____

_____

_____

List 10 things you are grateful for today.

_____

_____

_____

_____

_____

_____

_____

_____

_____

Anger

YOUR GRATITUDE STORY: When has anger caused you to hurt someone? Did you ask for forgiveness?

_____

_____

_____

_____

_____

_____

_____

_____

_____

List 10 things you are grateful for today.

_____

_____

_____

_____

_____

_____

_____

_____

A Time To Remain Silent

YOUR GRATITUDE STORY: What do you do when you are hounded by questions that seemingly have no answers?

_____

_____

_____

_____

_____

_____

_____

_____

_____

_____

List 10 things you are grateful for today.

_____

_____

_____

_____

_____

_____

_____

_____

_____

A Time To Speak

YOUR GRATITUDE STORY: List five little miracles that have occurred in your life over the last five years.

_____

_____

_____

_____

_____

_____

_____

_____

_____

List 10 things you are grateful for today.

_____

_____

_____

_____

_____

_____

_____

_____

_____

A Lap Desk

YOUR GRATITUDE STORY: Think of one negative that you can turn into a positive by trying something different.

_____

_____

_____

_____

_____

_____

_____

_____

_____

List 10 things you are grateful for today.

_____

_____

_____

_____

_____

_____

_____

_____

_____

Kindergarten Books

YOUR GRATITUDE STORY: What is one thing you could do for a person who can't read?

_____

_____

_____

_____

_____

_____

_____

_____

_____

List 10 things you are grateful for today.

_____

_____

_____

_____

_____

_____

_____

_____

_____

Day 109

A Good Gynecologic Exam

YOUR GRATITUDE STORY: Who is your favorite doctor? The next time you visit, let them know why they are your favorite. If you want to multiply your blessings, do something nice for the staff.

_____

_____

_____

_____

_____

_____

_____

_____

_____

List 10 things you are grateful for today.

_____

_____

_____

_____

_____

_____

_____

_____

_____

Day 110

A Meaningful Thanksgiving

YOUR GRATITUDE STORY: List five things you can do to make every day a "thanksgiving" day.

_____

_____

_____

_____

_____

_____

_____

_____

_____

List 10 things you are grateful for today.

_____

_____

_____

_____

_____

_____

_____

_____

_____

Wonder

YOUR GRATITUDE STORY: List three of your favorite movies and why they were worth two hours of your time.

_____

_____

_____

_____

_____

_____

_____

_____

_____

List 10 things you are grateful for today.

_____

_____

_____

_____

_____

_____

_____

_____

Mama, I Remember Your Name

YOUR GRATITUDE STORY: If you had to choose between following your brain and following your heart, which would you choose? Why?

_____

_____

_____

_____

_____

_____

_____

_____

_____

List 10 things you are grateful for today.

_____

_____

_____

_____

_____

_____

_____

_____

_____

Reading, Writing, And Arithmetic

YOUR GRATITUDE STORY: What was your favorite subject in school? Would it be your favorite if you couldn't read?

_____

_____

_____

_____

_____

_____

_____

_____

_____

_____

List 10 things you are grateful for today.

_____

_____

_____

_____

_____

_____

_____

_____

_____

"Thank You" Christmas Cards

YOUR GRATITUDE STORY: What was your favorite Christmas toy when you were a child? Why was it your favorite?

_____

_____

_____

_____

_____

_____

_____

_____

_____

List 10 things you are grateful for today.

_____

_____

_____

_____

_____

_____

_____

My Brain And My Heart: A Good Mix

YOUR GRATITUDE STORY: List three of the most meaningful gifts you've received as an adult. Why were they so meaningful? List three of the most meaningful gifts you've ever given. How did giving them make you feel?

_____

_____

_____

_____

_____

_____

_____

_____

List 10 things you are grateful for today.

_____

_____

_____

_____

_____

_____

_____

_____

_____

_____

Day 116

Priceless Christmas Gifts

YOUR GRATITUDE STORY: Do you have a Christmas tradition? Write about it.

_____

_____

_____

_____

_____

_____

_____

_____

_____

List 10 things you are grateful for today.

_____

_____

_____

_____

_____

_____

_____

_____

A Year Of Miracles

Miracles occur where the invisible possibilities of life unfold as realities.
-Bernie Siegal, M.D.

YOUR GRATITUDE STORY: List at least three miracles that have occurred in your life.

_____

_____

_____

_____

_____

_____

_____

_____

List 10 things you are grateful for today.

_____

_____

_____

_____

_____

_____

_____

_____

_____

_____

I Fly

Shedding my cocoon, I am no longer dormant
no longer fearing life, death, success, failure
my striking colors slowly emerge
unveiling my soul, my being.
My hot pink untamed spirit begets beauty
the shine of my camouflaged wings distinguishes me.
My burnt orange razor sharp tongue
sinks deep into the throat of flowers
sipping the nectar that keeps my delicate body alive.
My sunflower thoughts, mixed with ocean blue feelings
flutter above fields of green and yellow.
Pregnant, I give rise to new butterflies.
Gracefully soaring over nature's bounty by day,
napping by the light of the moon at night
I am a butterfly.
Free to fly. Free to be me. Free to soar
Come fly with me. Life is short.

Myrtle D. Russell © 2019